SHANGHAI
COMMON EXPRESSIONS

Dunwoody Press/Wheaton, Maryland
1988

© Copyright 1988 by MRM. Inc.

All rights reserved. No part of the material protected by this copyright notice may be reproduced or utilized in any form or by any means, electronic or mechanical, including photocopying, recording, or by an information storage and retrieval system, without written permission from the copyright owner.

All questions and inquires should be directed to:
Dunwoody Press, Box 1825, Wheaton, MD 20902

First edition: 1988
87 88 89 90 91 5 4 3 2 1

Printed in the United States of America

Library of Congress Catalog Card Number: 88-051589

ISBN 0-931745-38-1

TABLE OF CONTENTS

PREFACE..v

LESSON 1: WORDS AND EXPRESSIONS FOR EVERYDAY USE......................1
    Part 1: Greetings...1
    Part 2: Introducing People..3
    Part 3: Studying..6
    Part 4: Conversation..8
    Part 5: Dates and Times...10
    Part 6: Talking about the Weather..12

LESSON 2: ENTERING A COUNTRY..14
    Part 1: At the Airport...14
    Part 2: Going Through Entry Formalties...16

LESSON 3: AT THE HOTEL...19

LESSON 4: SHOPPING...22
    Part 1: At A Department Store...22
    Part 2: At An Arts and Crafts Shop...25
    Part 3: At A Fruit Store...27
    Part 4: At The Foreign Language Bookstore......................................28

LESSON 5: MEALS..30

LESSON 6: AT THE POST AND TELECOMMUNICATONS OFFICE.............33
    Part 1: Mailing a Letter..33
    Part 2: Posting a Parcel...35
    Part 3: Sending a Telegram..36

LESSON 7: MAKING TELEPHONE CALLS..37
    Part 1: Local Telephone Calls...37
    Part 2: Long-Distance Telephone Calls..39

LESSON 8: VISITING THE DOCTOR..40
    Part 1: Becoming Ill..40
    Part 2: At The Hospital's Registrar Office...41
    Part 3: In the Consulting Room...42
    Part 4: Filling A Prescription And Having An Injection........................45

LESSON 9: GOING TO THE BANK 47
   Part 1: Exchanging Money..47
   Part 2: Depositing and Drawing Money..49

LESSON 10: ASKING THE WAY AND GOING BY PUBLIC TRANSPORTATION..50
   Part 1: Asking The Way..50
   Part 2: On The Bus..52
   Part 3: Taking a Taxi..54

LESSON 11: AT THE BARBERSHOP AND THE CLEANERS...................56
   Part 1: At The Barber's Shop...57
   Part 2: At The Cleaner's...58

LESSON 12: AT THE PHOTO STUDIO..60

LESSON 13: SIGHTSEEING..61
   Part 1: Sentences Commonly Used in Sightseeing.........................61
   Part 2: Touring Shanghai..63

LESSON 14: ENTERTAINMENT AND RECREATION..............................65
   Part 1: Going to See Beijing Opera...65
   Part 2: Going To The Movies..68
   Part 3: Watching Television 69

LESSON 15: TRAVELING..71
   Part 1: Going Through The Formalities of Traveling......................71
   Part 2: Traveling by Train..73
   Part 3: Traveling by Ship..75
   Part 4: Traveling by Plane...76

LESSON 16: LEAVE-TAKING..78
   Part 1: At A Farewell Banquet..78
   Part 2: Saying Good-bye At The Airport...81

PREFACE

This volume was developed using the *600 Practical Chinese Sentences** as a model. The purpose of this book is to present colloquial Shanghai sentences in a manner that will enable English speakers to learn the phrases necessary for visiting Shanghai. The book is accompanied by a set of cassette tapes for those who wish to study without an instructor.

Each of the sentence entries consists of an English sentence followed by the corresponding sentence spoken slowly in colloquial Shanghai dialect. There is a pause to allow the learner to say the Shanghai sentence. The sentence is then repeated in colloquial Shanghai dialect at a normal conversational rate, followed by another pause to allow the learner to say it again. The recorded sentences conform to the sequence and numbering in the book.

*600 Practical Chinese Sentences, Zhang Yajun, et. al. Shanghai, Shanghai Education Publishing House 1981, 154 p.

ACKNOWLEDGEMENTS

Dunwoody Press wishes to acknowledge with gratitude the following who have made the publication of this work possible:

- Chen Yinzhang and Zhai Xiangjun for converting the original Chinese sentences into Wu
- Chen Yinzhang for the Shanghai renditions heard on the tapes
- Tom Creamer for the English glosses heard on the tapes
- Zhai Xiangjun for writing out the Chinese characters in the text
- Richang Lu for arranging the production of the transcription
- Hua Hung and Wei Xian for their transcription of the text
- Glenda Duncan for the typesetting of the manuscript
- Harry Goff for the layout of the manuscript

JDM/dz

LESSON 1

WORDS AND EXPRESSIONS FOR EVERYDAY USE
日 常 用 语

Part 1

Greetings
问 候

1. Hello! How do you do?
   侬好!

2. Good morning!
   侬早!

3. Good morning!
   早上好!

4. Good evening!
   晚上好!

5. I'm very happy to be in China.
   到中国来,我邪气开心。

6. This is my first visit to China.
   我是第一次来中国。

7. How are you?
   侬身体哪能?

1

8. I'm very well, and you?
   我身体交关好,侬呢?

9. I'm very well, too.
   我也交关好。

10. Are you busy with your work?
    侬工作忙哦?

11. Not too busy. (Very busy.)
    勿大忙。(交关忙。)

12. We haven't seen each other for a long time.
    阿拉有交关辰光嬺没碰面了。

13. How is Anna?
    安娜好哦?

14. She is very well. Anna asked me to give you her regards.
    伊蛮好。安娜叫我问侬问好。

15. Thanks.
    谢谢。

16. Good-bye.
    再会。

Part 2

Introducing People
介绍

17. What's your family name?
侬姓啥？

18. My family name is Wang.
我姓王。

19. What's your personal name?
侬叫啥名字？

20. My personal name is Tom.
我叫汤姆。

21. Who is this gentleman?
迪位先生是啥人？

22. This is my friend, Professor Ball.
伊是我格朋友，鲍尔教授。

23. Is that Mrs. Rogers?
迪个阿是罗杰斯夫人？

24. No, she isn't. (Yes, she is.)
勿是。（是格。）

25. Sorry.
对勿起。

26. It doesn't matter.
    呒没关系。

27. May I introduce Mr. Shaw, the manager of a publishing house.
    我来交侬介绍一下,迪位是出版社经理肖先生。

28. Let me introduce myself. My name is Zhang Peng.
    我来自我介绍一下吧,我叫张朋。

29. Here is my calling card.
    迪个是我格名片。

30. I'm very glad to meet you.
    看到侬邪气开心。

31. What country are you from?
    侬是阿里一个国家格人?

32. I'm Canadian.
    我是加拿大人。

33. Do you speak English?
    侬会得讲英文哦?

34. I speak English but not French.
    我会讲英文,不过,我勿会得讲法文格。

35. Do you know Chinese?
    侬会得讲中文哦?

36. A little, but I don't speak very well.
会得一眼眼，讲得勿大好。

37. Do you understand my Chinese?
我讲中文，侬听得懂哦？

38. Yes, I do. (No, I don't.)
我听得懂。(我听勿懂。)

39. I beg your pardon, will you please say it again?
对勿起，请侬再讲一遍。

40. Please speak a little slower.
请侬讲慢一眼。

41. Please write it down.
请侬写下来。

42. Can you say it in English?
侬可以用英文讲哦？

43. What do you call this in Chinese?
请问，迪个末事中文叫啥？

44. How do you say this in Chinese?
请问，迪句闲话用中文哪能讲？

45. My Chinese is rather poor. I'll be very glad if you could help me out.
我格中文推板来西，请多多指教。

Part 3

Studying
学 习

46. You speak very good Chinese.
侬格中文讲得蛮嗲。

47. Not at all.
勿来三,勿来三。

48. How long have you been studying Chinese?
侬中文学了几化辰光了?

49. I've just started.
我刚刚才开始。

50. I've been studying for more than three years.
我已经学了三年多了。

51. What school are you attending?
侬现在垃拉阿里一个学堂读书?

52. I'm studying at Fudan University.
我垃拉复旦大学读书。

53. Do you find the Chinese language difficult?
侬觉着中文难哦?

54. Not very difficult, but I think Chinese characters are very difficult.
勿大难,不过我觉着中文字蛮难格。

55. How many classes do you have each week?

侬每个礼拜上几节课?

56. We have sixteen classes each week.

阿拉每个礼拜上十六节课。

57. Besides modern Chinese, what else do you study?

除脱现代汉语之外,侬还学眼啥?

58. We also study Chinese history.

阿拉还学中国历史。

59. Sometimes we listen to broadcasts in Chinese.

有格辰光,阿拉还听中文广播。

60. Can you follow broadcasts in Chinese?

侬听得懂中文广播哦?

61. I don't understand them yet. (Not yet. I can only get a general idea.)

现在还听勿懂。(勿来三,我只能听懂大概格意思。)

Part 4

Conversation

交 谈

62. Come in, please.

请进!

63. Sit down, please.
请坐！

64. Have some tea.
请吃茶！

65. Where is your home?
侬格屋里垃拉啥地方？

66. I live in Washington.
我格屋里垃拉华盛顿。

67. Do you have a large family?
请问，侬屋里还有眼啥人？

68. I have a father, mother and a younger sister.
我屋里还有阿爸、姆妈搭之妹妹。

69. Where does your father work?
侬阿爸垃拉阿里工作？

70. He works in a bank.
伊垃拉银行里工作。

71. How old are you?
侬今年几岁？

72. I am thirty-one years old.
我今年三十一岁。

73. Are you married?

侬结婚了哦？

74. Yes, I'm married. (No, I'm not married yet.)

我结婚了。(我还呒没结婚。)

75. What does your wife do?

侬爱人做啥工作？

76. She is a middle-school teacher.

伊是中学里向格老师。

77. How many children do you have?

侬有几个小人？

78. I have two children, a son and a daughter.

我有两个小人，一个儿子，一个囡囡。

Part 5

Dates And Time

日脚搭之辰光

79. What's the date today?

今朝是几号？

80. Today is the nineteenth.

今朝是十九号。

81. What day of the week is it today?

今朝是礼拜几?

82. Today is Saturday.

今朝是礼拜六。

83. Today is Saturday, May 19th, 1984.

今朝是一九八四年五月十九号,礼拜六。

84. What time is it?

现在几点钟了?

85. It's eight o'clock.

现在八点钟。

86. When did you arrive in Shanghai?

侬是啥辰光到上海格?

87. I arrived in Shanghai at half past three yesterday afternoon.

我是昨日下半日三点半到上海格。

88. What plans do you have for this morning?

今朝上半日侬有啥个安排哦?

89. I plan to meet a friend of mine at ten.

十点钟格辰光我要会见一个朋友。

90. When are you leaving?

侬啥个辰光离开格搭?

91. I haven't made up my mind yet. I plan to leave at the end of this month or the beginning of the next month.

现在还呒没定下来。我准备拉拉迪个月底或者下个月初离开格搭。

Part 6

Talking About the Weather
天 气

92. It's raining (snowing).

落雨(雪)了。

93. It's stopped raining (snowing).

雨(雪)停了。

94. It's very cold (hot) today.

今朝佬冷(热)格。

95. It's a fine day today.

今朝天气交关好。

96. It's getting warmer every day.

天气越来越热了。

97. What's the temperature today?

今朝格气温是几度?

98. It's twenty-four degrees Centigrade today.

今朝格气温是摄氏廿四度。

11

99. What's the weather going to be like tomorrow?
明朝格天气哪能?

100. The weather forecast says it will be cloudy and there will be rain at times.
气象预报报道,明朝阴天,有辰光有雨。

101. Will it be windy tomorrow?
明朝有勿有风?

102. It will be a bit windy tomorrow. There will be a northwesterly wind, measuring about two and three on the Beaufort Scale.
明朝有点小风,风力两到三级,风向西北。

103. Have you gotten used to the weather in Shanghai?
侬对上海格气候适应哦?

104. Yes, it's O.K. The weather in Shanghai is similar to Tokyo's.
还可以,上海格气候搭之东京差勿多。

105. They say it's very cold in the winter in Beijing, isn't it?
听说,北京格冬天邪气冷,是哦?

106. Yes, in the winter it's colder in Beijing than in Shanghai.
是格,北京格冬天比上海冷。

LESSON 2

ENTERING A COUNTRY
入　境
Part 1

At The Airport
垃拉机场上

107. I came from America.

    我是从美国来格。

108. I have come to China as a tourist.

    我是到中国来旅游格。

109. Sorry to trouble you, may I ask you a question?

    麻烦侬，请问侬一桩事体好哦？

110. What is it? Please go ahead and ask.

    啥个事体？侬问好了。

111. How can I get in touch with the Chinese People's Association for Friendship with Foreign Countries?

    哪能介搭之中国人民对外友好协会取得联系？

112. I want to go to a hotel. Are there any taxis here? (Is there a bus service here?)

    我想到旅馆去，迪搭有出租汽车（公共汽车）哦？

113. Can you help me to find the International Travel Service people?

    侬帮我寻一寻国际旅行社格人好哦？

114. Wait a moment, please.
请稍微等一歇。

115. I'm from the International Travel Service. Welcome to China.
我是国际旅行社格,欢迎侬到中国来。

116. It's very kind of you to meet me.
谢谢侬来接我。

117. It's a pleasure to have this opportunity to come to China.
我能有机会到中国来,心里向邪气开心。

118. How was the journey?
侬一路上好哦?

119. Excellent, everything went very well.
交关好,一切才佬顺利格。

120. Have all your things arrived?
侬格行李才到齐了哦?

121. Let's have a short rest before going through the formalities.
阿拉休息一歇就去办手续。

122. O.K.
好格。

Part 2

Going Through Entry Formalities
办理入境手续

123. Could I see your vaccination certificate, please?
请侬拿侬个预防接种证书拨我看看。

124. Here you are.
喏。

125. Your vaccination certificate is valid.
侬格证书是有效格。

126. Your vaccination certificate is no longer valid. You must have another vaccination.
侬格证书已经过期了。侬还要再打一针。

127. Your passport, please.
侬格护照呢?

128. How long do you plan to stay in China?
侬打算垃拉中国蹲几化辰光?

129. I'm going to stay about three weeks.
我打算蹲三个礼拜左右。

130. I've come for the Chinese Export Commodities Fair.
我是来参加中国出品商品交易会格。

131. Please fill out this Luggage Declaration.
请侬拿迪份行李物品申报单填一填。

132. Could you tell me how to fill in this part?
请问,迪个一栏哪能填法?

133. Is this right?
迪能介填对勿对?

134. I'd like you to get an interpreter for me.
我想请侬寻一个翻译来。

135. Do you have anything to declare?
侬有啥末事要申报哦?

136. Do you have any foreign currency?
侬有外汇哦?

137. I have some American dollars.
我有一眼美元。

138. I have a laissez-passer.
我有免验证。

139. The import (export) of these articles is prohibited.
迪些末事是禁止带入(带出)格。

140. All this luggage is mine.
迪些行李才是我格。

141. Do you mind opening this suitcase? I'd like to have a look.
请侬拿迪只皮箱打开,我要看一看。

142. All these things are for my personal use.
迪点末事才是我自家用格。

143. Those are gifts for friends.
伊些末事是送拨朋友格礼品。

144. What is in this box?
迪只盒子里装格是啥末事?

145. According to the regulations, you must pay duty on these things.
根据规定,迪些末事一定要上税。

146. How much duty should I pay?
请问,我应该上几化税?

147. Do you have any prohibited items with you?
侬是否带了违禁品?

148. I have nothing that is prohibited.
我一眼违禁品也呒没带。

149. May I close the bags now?
我可以拿迪只皮箱关起来了哦?

150. All right. Sorry to have troubled you.
可以,麻烦侬了。

LESSON 3

AT THE HOTEL
拉旅馆里

151. Have you any vacant rooms?
 佣迪搭有空房间哦？

152. What kind of room would you like to have?
 侬想要哪能价格房间？

153. I'd like to have the best (cheapest) single (double) room.
 我想要一个顶好格单人房间（顶便宜格双人房间）

154. What is the price for the room?
 房钿是几化？

155. Do you want a deposit?
 要不要先交钞票？

156. Have you reserved your room?
 侬格房间订好了哦？

157. Which delegation are you with?
 侬是阿里一个代表团格？

158. I'm a member of the touring party.
 我是旅行团格人。

169. Where is the power socket?
电源插头垃拉啥个地方?

170. Oh, I've left the key in my room.
哎呀!我格钥匙忘记拉房间里了。

171. Are there any telegrams (letters) for me today?
今朝有我格电报(信)哦?

172. If somebody asks for me, please tell him that I'll be back in an hour.
假如有人来寻我,请侬告诉伊,我一个钟头之内转来。

173. Wake me up at five tomorrow morning, please.
请明朝早上五点钟叫醒我。

174. Sorry to trouble you, but could you call a taxi for me?
麻烦侬,帮我喊一部出租汽车。

175. I'm checking out. Can I have my bill, please?
我要走了,请帮我结结账。

176. I'll be back in two weeks. Can you take care of my luggage for me?
我半个号头之后再转来,侬帮我代看一下行李好哦?

177. Please forward my letters to this address.
请拿我格信转到迪个地址。

LESSON 4

SHOPPING
买末事

Part 1
At A Department Store
垃拉百货商店

178. I want to buy this.

我要买迪个末事。

179. Can you direct me to the department selling black tea (jasmine tea, green tea)?

请侬指拨我看看,阿里格柜台是卖红茶(花茶、绿茶)格?

180. Do you have any ivory chopsticks (seals)?

俫迪搭有卖象牙筷子(图章)哦?

181. How much is a jin (a meter, a bottle)?

几钿一斤(一公尺、一瓶)?

182. Can you write its price on a piece of paper for me, please?

请侬拿价钿写拉纸头上好哦?

183. It's too expensive.

太贵了。

184. Have you anything cheaper (bigger, smaller, stronger)?

有勿有便宜(大、小、牢)一眼格?

185. Can you show me a selection to choose from?

请多拿几只出来，让我捡捡看好哦？

186. Can I change this, please?

请帮我调一只好哦？

187. All right. That's all I want.

迪点够了。

188. I don't want it (them). Thank you.

我勿买，谢谢依。

189. Excuse me, but could you show me a pair of cotton shoes?

对勿起，让我看看伊双布鞋子好哦？

190. What size do you take?

侬穿几码？

191. I probably take a size 26.

大概是廿六码。

192. Can I try them on?

让我穿穿看好哦？

193. This pair does not fit. It's a bit too tight (big).

迪双鞋子勿大合适，有眼紧（大）。

194. Have you any other styles (colors)?

别格样子（颜色）格有哦？

21

195. Do you like this color?
迪种颜色侬看哪能?

196. Fine, I'll take this pair.
蛮好,我就买迪双。

197. Give me a receipt, please.
请开张发票。

198. Please pay at the desk over there.
请到伊面边去付钞票。

199. Please wrap it up.
麻烦侬帮我包一包好哦?

Part 2

At An Arts And Crafts Shop
垃拉工艺美术商店

200. I am especially interested in Chinese arts and crafts.
我对中国格工艺美术品邪气感兴趣。

201. I want to buy some souvenirs of China to take home.
我想买点中国格纪念品带转去。

202. What are the famous local products here?
迪搭有点啥个土特产?

203. Excuse me, can you tell me what this is?
对勿起,迪个是啥末事?

204. May I have a look at that tea set?
伊套茶具让我看看好哦?

205. I want to buy Chinese embroideries, could you recommend some for me?
我想买点中国格刺绣,侬觉得阿里一种好?

206. In our shop, we have embroideries from Hunan, Hangzhou and Suzhou. All of them are very famous.
阿拉店里有湖南、杭州、苏州格刺绣,才是邪气有名格。

207. It's really beautiful, and typically Chinese.
绣得真斩,是地地道道格中国风格。

208. By the way, may I ask where I can buy some papercuts?
顺便问一声,啥地方可以买到剪纸?

209. At that counter over there.
垃拉伊面边格柜台。

Part 3

At A Fruit Store
拉拉水果店

210. What can I do for you?
侬要买啥？

211. I'm just having a look.
随便看看。

212. The grapes look very nice. Are they sweet?
迪点葡萄看工去倒蛮灵格，勿晓得甜哦？

213. Yes, would you like some?
蛮甜格，想买一眼哦？

214. I'll take three jin.
买三斤。

215. Anything else?
还要一点别格末事哦？

216. Two jin of pears, please. How much is it altogether?
再买两斤生梨，一共几钿？

217. That'll be two yuan and sixty fen.
一共两块六角。

218. Yours is a five yuan note, so your change is two yuan and forty fen.
迪个是五块头,找侬两块四角。

219. Are you sure there is no mistake in the bill? Would you check it please?
侬是否算错脱了,再算一遍好哦?

Part 4
At The Foreign Language Bookstore
垃拉外文书店

220. Comrade. do you have any Chinese conversation handbooks for foreigners (tourists)?
同志,有勿有为外国人(旅游者)编写格中文会话手册?

221. I'd like a Chinese-English one.
我要中英对照本。

222. There is a book entitled "600 Practical Chinese Sentences". Too bad, they're sold out.
有一本《实用汉语600句》,不过,侬来得太勿巧了,已经卖光了。

223. Oh, what shall I do?
哎呀,格哪能办?

224. This one is called "Spoken Chinese". It's quite good too. Do have a look at it.
迪本《汉语口语》也蛮灵格。侬翻翻看。

225. Well, it looks quite useful.

嗯，蛮灵格。

226. When was it published, and by whom?

阿里一年出版格？阿里一个出版社出版格？

227. Who is the author?

作者是啥人？

228. This is Part One. Part Two will probably come out in two months.

迪个是上册，下册大概垃拉两个号头之后再出版。

229. This is a bestseller.

迪个是一本畅销书。

230. Do you want the hardcover or the paperback edition?

侬要精装本，还是平装本？

231. I'll take five of each.

我每样要五本。

232. Have you any books on Chinese acupuncture?

㑚有关于中国针灸格书哦？

233. Wait a minute, please. I'll go and have a look.

等一歇，我去寻寻看。

234. Sorry, there are none in English. For the Chinese editions, you'd better try at the Xinhua Bookstore.

对勿起，只有中文版，呒没英文版。侬最好到新华书店去看看。

LESSON 5

MEALS
用餐

235. I'm hungry.
我肚皮饿了。

236. Can you recommend a good restaurant here?
请问,迪搭阿里一爿饭店顶好?

237. What would you like to have, Chinese food or Western food?
侬想吃中餐还是西餐?

238. I'd like to try Chinese food.
我想尝尝中餐。

239. I want to try your local specialities.
我想尝尝俩迪搭几只有名格菜。

240. Oh, the Yangzhou Restaurant is by far the best here.
扬州饭店是迪搭顶有名气格。

241. Excuse me, is this table reserved?
对勿起,迪只台子有人哦?

242. May I have the menu?
请拿菜单拨我看看好哦?

243. Please recommend some dishes to us.
请帮阿拉点几只菜好哦?

244. I don't like meat.
我不欢喜吃肉。

245. I like vegetables.
我欢喜吃蔬菜。

246. I'll take the baked, crispy yellow fish and assorted vegetables.
请来一只红烧黄鱼,和一盘素什锦。

247. Not too salty, please.
勿要太咸。

248. What's that dish?
伊面是只啥个菜?

249. It's an assorted cold dish, with sliced sausages and preserved eggs. Would you like to order one?
伊面是只拼盘,里向有香肠、皮蛋,来一盘好哦?

250. Would you like some soup?
侬汤要哦?

251. What would you like to drink?
侬要吃啥个酒?

252. Two bottles of beer, please.
来两瓶啤酒。

253. We are in a hurry, please rush our order.
阿拉有点急事体，菜是否能快点来？

254. It's delicious. It really lives up to its reputation.
味道蛮好，真是名不虚传。

255. Can I reserve four places for eight o'clock tomorrow evening?
我要订明朝夜里八点钟格四只位子。

256. We'd like four dishes and a soup.
要四菜一汤。

257. May I have the bill?
请拿账算一算。

258. Please keep the change.
多下来格找头，侬收下来好了。

259. We don't accept tips. Thank you just the same.
谢谢，阿拉是勿收小费格。

LESSON 6

AT THE POST AND TELECOMMUNICATIONS OFFICE
拉拉邮电局

Part 1

Mailing A Letter
寄 信

260. Excuse me, but could you tell me where the nearest post office is?
请问,迪搭附近邮局有哦?

261. What's the postage on this letter to Rome, please?
迪封信寄到罗马,要贴几化邮票?

262. Do you wish to send it as an ordinary or registered letter?
侬要寄平信,还是挂号信?

263. I want to send this letter by registered air mail.
我要寄航空挂号信.

264. Let me weigh your letter.
让我称一称。

265. The letter is three grams overweight. The postage will be one yuan.
迪封信超重三克,要贴一块洋钿格邮票.

266. How long will it take to reach Rome?
迪封信到罗马要几天?

267. Five days or so.
五天左右。

268. Can you give me two sets of commemorative stamps, please?
我想买两套纪念邮票。

269. Which do you prefer? Choose whichever ones you like.
侬欢喜阿里一种,自己捡好了。

270. I'd like one set of each of these stamps, and ten envelopes.
迪个几种邮票每样要一套,另外再要十只信封。

Part 2

Posting a Parcel

寄包裹

271. Where does one send (pick up) parcels?

    寄(领)包裹垃拉啥地方？

272. I want to send this parcel to Marseilles.

    我想拿迪只包裹寄到马赛去。

273. What are you sending?

    侬寄格是啥末事？

274. Sorry, according to our regulations, it is prohibited to send this kind of Chinese medicine out of China.

    对勿起，根据我国规定，迪种中药是不准寄到国外去格。

275. I'm sorry. I didn't know.

    对勿起，我勿晓得。

276. You can't pack it that way, please put it in a wooden box, otherwise it's very likely to break.

    侬迪能格包装是不来三格。侬应该拨伊装垃木头盒子里，否则要碰坏脱格。

277. May I address it in French?

    包裹上格地名、人名用法文写来三哦？

278. Certainly, but be sure to write the names and the addresses of the recipient and the sender clearly.

当然来三。收格人搭之寄格人格地址交名字一定要写清爽。

Part 3

Sending A Telegram
拍电报

279. Excuse me, can I send a telegram here?

对勿起,迪搭可以拍电报哦?

280. No, at the counter marked No. 4, please.

勿可以,拍电报请到四号窗口。

281. I want to send an ordinary (urgent) telegram to Guangzhou. Please give me a telegram form.

我要拍一只,普通(加急)电报到广州。请拨我一张电报稿纸好哦?

282. How much do you charge for each word?

请问,一个字要几钿?

283. Three fen per word in Chinese, three fen per word in English.

中文每个字三分,英文每个词三分。

284. Tell me, please, when will this telegram arrive?

迪份电报啥个辰光可以到?

LESSON 7

MAKING TELEPHONE CALLS
打 电 话

Part 1

Local Telephone Calls
市 内 电 话

285. Is there a public telephone nearby?
请问，迪搭附近公用电话有哦？

286. May I use this phone?
迪只电话我可以用一用哦？

287. Is this a house phone? Can I call outside?
迪个是内线电话还是外线电话？

288. What should I do if I want to call an outside line?
哪能介打外线电话？

289. Please dial "0" first.
先拨"0"。

290. Hello, is that Fudan University?
喂，哪是复旦大学，是哦？

291. No, you have the wrong number.
勿是，依打错脱了。

292. Is that Fudan University? Extension 19, please.

侬是复旦大学,是哦?请转19分机。

293. The line is busy. Call back in a minute, please.

请等一歇再打,现在有人拉拉打。

294. Who are you calling?

侬打拨啥人?

295. May I speak to Mr. Muller, a West German student?

我打拨西德学生米勒。

296. Who's speaking, please?

侬是啥人?

297. This is Paul speaking.

我是保罗。

298. All right, please hold. Don't hang up.

好,请侬等一等,勿要拿电话挂脱。

299. He isn't in, please phone again later.

伊勿拉拉海。侬等一歇再打来好哦?

300. Give me your phone number and I'll ask him to call you back.

请拿侬格电话号码告诉我,我叫伊交侬打回电。

Part 2

Long-Distance Telephone Calls
长途电话

301. I'd like to make a long-distance call to Chicago.

我要挂一只到芝加哥格长途电话。

302. How long will it take to get through?

要等多少辰光才能接通?

303. Could you hurry up with the long-distance call to Chicago?

帮我催一催到芝加哥格长途电话好哦?

304. The long-distance call to Chicago has come through. Please use Booth No. 5.

到芝加哥格长途电话接通了,请到五号隔音室去打。

305. I can't hear you very well. Please speak a little louder.

我听勿大清爽,请侬讲得响一点。

306. We've been disconnected. Could you put the call through again?

电话断脱了,请侬再帮我接通好哦?

307. You spoke for five minutes. That will be forty-eight yuan in all.

侬讲了五分钟,电话费一共四十八块。

LESSON 8

VISITING THE DOCTOR
看 医 生

Part 1

Becoming Ill
生 毛 病

308. I'm ill.

   我生毛病了。

309. I'm seriously ill.

   我格毛病邪气利害。

310. I don't feel very well today.

   今朝我勿大适意。

311. I must see a doctor (stay in a hospital for an examination).

   我要去看医生（住院检查）。

312. Can you send for a doctor (an ambulance), please?

   侬帮我请一丁医生来好哦？

   侬帮我叫一部救护车来好哦？

313. Can you come with me to the hospital, please?

   侬陪我到医院去一趟好哦？

314. O.K. I'll take you there.
好格，我陪侬去。

Part 2

At The Hospital's Registrar Office
垃拉挂号处

315. Excuse me, is this the place to register?
对勿起，挂号是勿是垃拉迪搭？

316. Which department do you want?
侬要挂啥个科？

317. I want the Medical Department (Surgical Department, Eye, Nose, Throat Department, Department of Gynecology).
我要挂内科（外科、五官科、妇科）。

318. Do you have your registration card with you?
侬挂号卡带了哦？

319. This is my first time here.
我是第一次来迪搭看毛病。

320. Sorry, I forgot to bring it.
对勿起，我忘记脱带了。

321. This is your registration card. Please bring it along the next time you come for treatment.
迪个是侬格挂号卡，下趟来看毛病请带得来。

322. Which room do I go to?
我到几号房间去看病?

323. Go to Room No. 8, please.
请到八号房间去.

Part 3

In The Consulting Room
垃拉诊断室里

324. What's bothering you?
侬阿里搭不适宜.

325. I have a headache and fever. I can't eat anything and I feel weak all over.
我头疼, 发寒热, 吃不落饭, 浑身呒没力气.

326. I have a stomach-ache (toothache, earache).
我肚皮(牙齿、耳朵)疼.

327. I've sprained my arm.
我格手骨别筋了.

328. My heart trouble has recurred.
我格心脏病发了.

329. How long have you been feeling like this?
有多少辰光了?

330. It began yesterday. (Several days ago.)
从昨日开始格(已经有好几天了)。

331. Let me take your temperature first. Please put this thermometer under your arm.
先量一量体温。拿体温表放垃拉胳肢下。

332. Show me your tongue, please.
舌头伸出来让我看看。

333. Please unbutton your coat and let me listen to your chest.
衣裳钮子解开来,让我听听侬格心脏。

334. Breathe deeply, please.
请深呼吸。

335. What diseases have you had in the past?
侬老早生过啥个毛病哦?

336. Have you ever had tuberculosis?
侬生过肺结核哦?

337. Does it hurt here?
迪搭疼哦?

338. Yes, it does. (No, it doesn't.)
疼格(勿疼)。

330. You need to have a blood (urine, stool) test.
侬去验验血（小便、大便）。

340. Please go to the X-ray room and have your chest X-rayed.
请到X光室去作肺部透视。

341. You'll have to make an electrocardiogram.
侬要作一个心电图。

342. Doctor, what's wrong with me?
医生，我生啥个毛病？

343. You are suffering from acute appendicitis and must have an operation at once.
侬生格是急性阑尾炎，要马上开刀。

344. I'm afraid it is the flu (pneumonia, enteritis).
侬恐怕得格是流行性感冒（肺炎、肠炎）。

345. Nothing serious, just take some medicine and have some injections, have a good rest and you'll be all right in a few days.
勿要紧，吃点药，打几针，好好休息，过两天就好了。

346. I don't like having injections. Could you give me some traditional Chinese medicine instead?
我勿想打针，顶好帮我开点中药。

347. O.K. Here is the prescription. You can get it filled at the dispensary.
可以，迪个是药方，侬到药房去拿药好了。

Part 4

Filling A Prescription And Having An Injection
拿药搭之打针

348. Excuse me, I'd like to have this prescription filled.
对勿起,我要拿药。

349. Here is your medicine. Take one dose of this mixture three times a day. Take two of these tablets twice a day - once in the morning, once in the evening.
迪个是侬格药。药水每天吃三次,每次一格。
药片每日吃两次,早上夜里各一次,每次两片。

350. You must not eat greasy food.
侬勿好吃油腻格末事。

351. You must not drink wine (strong coffee, strong tea).
侬勿好吃酒(吃浓咖啡,吃浓茶)。

352. This medicine is for external use, not to be taken orally.
迪个是外用药,当心勿要吃下去。

353. I'd like to have an injection.
我要打针。

354. You'd better have a test first, and wait 20 minutes to see if there is any reaction.
侬先作个试验,等廿分钟后,看看有啥反应。

355. I'm allergic to penicillin.

我打青霉素要过敏格。

356. Please come for another shot tomorrow.

明朝再来打一针。

LESSON 9

GOING TO THE BANK
到 银 行 去

Part 1

Exchanging Money
调 钞 票

357. Could you tell me where I can change my foreign currency?
请问，啥地方可以兑换外币？

358. What time does the Bank of China close?
中国银行几点钟关门？

359. I want to change these U.S. dollars into renminbi.
我想拿美元调成人民币。

360. What is the current rate of exchange between U.S. dollars and renminbi?
今朝美元搭之人民币格调价是多少？

361. Today it's 1 for 1.9.
今朝格调价是一比一点九。

362. Here are the foreign exchange certificates for the money you exchanged. Please check them.
迪个是侬调格外汇兑换券，请点点清爽。

363. Can you cash this traveler's check for me?

我要拿迪张旅行支票调现钞。

364. Here is my identification card.

迪个是我格身份证。

365. Sign your name here, please.

请垃拉格搭签个名。

366. Can you break a ten-yuan note?

侬能拿迪张十块头调成另格哦?

Part 2

Depositing And Drawing Money

存钞票搭之领钞票

367. Excuse me, I want to deposit some money.

对勿起,我要存点钞票。

368. Do you want to deposit your money in a current or in a fixed account?

侬要存活期还是定期?

369. What is the interest on a fixed deposit account?

定期格利息是几化?

370. 5.76 yuan per 100 yuan RMB a year.

一百块人民币一年格利息是五块七角六分。

371. I want to draw some money.
我要领点钞票。

372. Here is my bankbook.
迪个是我格存折。

373. How much do you want to take out?
侬领几化钞票?

374. I want to draw 500 yuan.
我要领五百块。

375. Please fill your name and the number of the account on this form.
请拿侬格名字搭之帐号填垃迪张表格里。

LESSON 10

ASKING THE WAY AND GOING BY PUBLIC TRANSPORTATION
问路搭之乘车

Part 1

Asking The Way
问 路

376. Could you tell me the way to the Friendship Store?
请问，到友谊商店哪能走？

377. Please turn east and go straight ahead.
朝东转弯一直往前走。

378. Turn right (left) at the traffic lights ahead.
走到前面红绿灯格地方朝右（左）打弯。

379. Is it far from here?
离开迪搭远哦？

380. No, it's only about 5 minutes' walk.
勿远，大约走五分钟就到了。

381. Excuse me. Is this the right way to the U.S. Consulate?
对勿起，到美国领事馆是走迪条路哦？

382. Could you tell me which bus goes to the Yu Garden?

请问,到城隍庙乘几路车?

383. Take trolley bus No. 26 to Yan'an Road, then transfer to the trolley bus No. 11. Get off at the terminus, and you'll be there.

侬先乘26路无轨电车到延安路,再调11路到终点站就到了。

384. Where is the stop for bus No. 57?

57路汽车站拉拉啥地方?

385. Cross the street, turn right, and you'll find it.

穿过迪条马路,朝右打弯就到了。

386. I'm lost. Where are we now?

我勿认得路了。阿拉现在拉拉啥地方?

387. Please draw a sketch and show me the way to People's Park.

请侬帮我画一张到人民公园去格路线图。

388. Please make a phone call to my hotel. The telephone number is 534242.

请侬打一只电话到我格旅馆去好哦?电话号码是534242。

389. Please take me to Jinjiang Hotel.

请侬送我到锦江饭店好哦?

Part 2

On The Bus
乘公共汽车

390. Does this bus go to the railway station?
请问,迪部汽车到火车站去哦?

391. Yes, it does. Get on, please.
去格,请上车.

392. Fares, please.
买票格有哦?

393. One ticket to No. 1 Department Store please.
我买一张到中百一店格车票.

394. Where did you get on?
侬是啥地方上来格?

395. I've just gotten on.
刚刚上来.

396. Please let me know when we get there.
麻烦侬,到站格辰光,请喊我一声.

397. Excuse me, what time does the last bus leave here?
请问,末班车几点钟开?

398. Usually it leaves the station at ten, on Saturdays and Sundays at eleven.

平常是十点钟,礼拜六交礼拜天是十一点钟。

399. The next stop is Xizang Road. Does anyone want to get off? If not, we won't stop.

下一站是西藏路,下车格有哦?呒没,就不停了。

400. This is No. 1 Department Store. You should get off now.

中百一店到了,侬可以下车了。

401. Excuse me, are you getting off here? If not, let's change places.

对勿起,侬下车哦?勿下,请让一让。

402. Let me off, please.

对勿起,我要下车。

Part 3

Taking A Taxi

乘出租汽车

403. Hello, is this the taxi company?

喂,哪是出租汽车公司哦?

404. I'd like a taxi.

我要一部出租汽车。

405. What's your address?

侬住垃啥地方?

406. Jinjiang Hotel, room number 125. My name is Tom.
锦江饭店, 125房间。我叫汤姆。

407. O.K., we'll be there in a minute.
好, 阿拉马上就来。

408. Where would you like to go?
侬要到啥个地方去?

409. Number 7 Lane 662, Huaihai Road, please.
淮海路662弄7号。

410. How long will it take?
到伊面要几化辰光?

411. About five minutes, I think.
大概五分钟。

412. Can we get there any quicker?
阿拉可以快点到哦?

413. I'm not sure, but I'll do my best.
吃勿准, 不过我可以尽量快一点。

414. Here we are. One yuan, five fen, please.
到了, 车费是一块另五分。

LESSON 11

AT THE BARBERSHOP AND THE CLEANER'S
剃头、汰衣裳

Part 1

At The Barber's Shop
拉拉理发店

415. Comrade, I'd like to have a haircut.
    同志,我要剃个头。

416. Yes, sit here please.
    好,请坐到迪搭来。

417. What can I do for you?
    侬想剃啥个式样?

418. Same as before.
    老样子。

419. Just a trim will do.
    稍微修一修就可以了。

420. Cut it a bit shorter, please.
    请剃得短一眼。

421. Not too much off, please.
    勿要剃脱太多。

422. Trim my moustache, please.
请帮我上面格胡子剪一剪。

423. Would you like a shave?
面修哦?

424. Not this time.
迪趟勿修了。

425. Give me a shampoo, please.
帮我汰汰头。

426. I'd like to have my hair dyed black.
我想把头发染成黑颜色。

427. Shall I put on some hair oil?
要勿要搽油?

428. No, but I'd like my hair dried.
勿要,吹吹干就可以了。

429. Give me a mirror, please.
请递拨我一面镜子好哦?

Part 2

At The Cleaner's
拉拉汰衣裳店

430. I want to have my shirt and trousers cleaned, please.
请拨迪件衬衫搭之裤子汰一汰。

431. Can woollen clothes be dry-cleaned in your shop?
傗格店可以干汰毛货衣裳哦?

432. Please remove the grease spot.
请拨迪块油渍汰脱。

433. The button has come off my overcoat, could you sew it on for me, please?
我格大衣钮子落脱了,请侬帮我钉一钉。

434. Is it possible to get this pressed?
迪件衣裳烫一烫来三哦?

435. When can I pick them up?
啥辰光可以来拿?

436. You can pick them up on the sixth.
侬六号来拿。

437. Is it possible for me to pick them up sooner? You see, I'm going to Guilin.
早一点来三哦?我要到桂林去。

55

438. Here is the receipt. Please keep it. You'll need it to get your clothes back.

请拿发票园好。拿衣裳格辰光要用格。

439. Do I have to pay right now?

现在我要付钞票哦?

440. No, not now. You can pay when you come to pick them up.

现在勿要,拿衣裳格辰光再付好了。

LESSON 12

AT THE PHOTO STUDIO
拉拉照相馆

441. Comrade, I'd like to have my picture taken.
 同志，我要拍照片。

442. How large? Half or full-length?
 侬想拍几化大格？半身还是全身？

443. I want to have a 2 inch full-face picture for a travel permit.
 我要拍旅行证上用格两寸正面照。

444. I want to have these rolls of films developed.
 我要冲胶卷。

445. What kind are they, color or black-and-white?
 啥个胶卷？彩色格还是黑白格？

446. They are all color, three 135's and one 120.
 全部是彩色格，三卷135，一卷120。

447. Do you want prints made?
 底片要勿要印？

448. Would you like to have them enlarged?
 要勿要放大？

449. Sure, if they come out well.
 照得好就放，勿好就算了。

57

LESSON 13

SIGHTSEEING
游览

Part 1

Sentences Commonly Used In Sightseeing
游览用语

450. I am told Guilin is a beautiful place with picturesque scenery.
听说桂林风景邪气嗲。

451. Please tell me some places worth visiting here.
请告诉我，阿里一些地方顶值得去白相格？

452. Could you tell me in detail (simply) the history of this ancient city, please?
请侬拿迪座古城格历史情况详细（简单）介绍介绍。

453. What is the name of this park?
迪座公园叫啥名字？

454. What building is that?
伊个是啥个建筑？

455. Whose statue is that?
伊个塑像是啥人？

456. How high is this palace?
迪座宫殿有几化高？

457. In what dynasty was this built?
迪个是哪里一个朝代造格?

458. When was this pagoda built?
迪座塔是啥辰光造格?

459. It was built around 1563, more than 400 years ago.
迪座塔是一五六三年造格,离开现在有四百多年了。

460. What are the stone animals for?
迪些石兽有啥用场?

461. Is the museum open now?
博物馆现在开放哦?

462. What time does the museum open?
博物馆啥个辰光开放?

463. How much is the admission fee?
门票要几钿?

464. Where did you get this souvenir badge?
侬迪个徽章是阿里买格?

465. Can I take photographs here?
迪搭可以拍照哦?

466. Let's take a photo here as a souvenir.
阿拉垃迪搭拍张照片,留个纪念好哦?

Part 2

Touring Shanghai
游览上海

467. How long have you been in Shanghai?
侬来上海有几化辰光了?

468. I have been in Shanghai for one week.
我已经来了一个礼拜了。

469. What places have you visited?
侬已经去过些啥地方?

470. I've been to the Bund and the Children's Palace.
我已经去过外滩搭之少年宫。

471. Have you visited the Yu Garden yet?
侬豫园去白相过了哦?

472. I wanted to go there yesterday, but I couldn't because I had something else to do.
我本来想昨日去格,结果有事体哞没去。

473. What a pity. You can't say you've been to Shanghai without seeing the Yu Garden.
到上海来哞到过豫园真是太可惜了。

474. That's true. Are there any other scenic spots and historical sites in Shanghai besides all of these?

格句闲话一眼不错。除脱迪些地方以外，上海还有点啥名胜古迹？

475. There are the Jade Buddha Temple, the Guyi Garden, the Lu Xun's Tomb Temple......there really are many other places worth visiting.

还有玉佛寺、古漪园、鲁迅墓……好白相格地方多了。

476. Really? I shall try and find time to visit them all.

真格？我一定要抽辰光去迪些地方白相相。

LESSON 14

ENTERTAINMENT AND RECREATION
文娱活动

Part 1

Going to See Beijing Opera
看京戏

477. Are you interested in Beijing Opera?

侬对中国格京戏感兴趣哦?

478. I've never seen it before. I've only seen some stage photos. I'll certainly go and see one during my stay in China.

吾没看过,只看到一点剧照。格趟到中国来,我一定要去看一看。

479. Shall we go and see Beijing Opera tonight?

今朝夜里阿拉去看京戏好哦?

480. That's wonderful. What is it we are going to see? Who is playing the leading role?

好极了。今朝做啥个戏?啥人主演?

481. The opera is called "The Battle of Hongzhou". Guan Sushuang is playing the leading role.

今朝做《战洪州》,是关肃霜主演格。

482. Where will it be?

拉拉啥地方做?

483. At the Liberation Theater.
 垃拉解放剧场。

484. Will you please tell me something about the story of this opera before it begins?
 趁现在还没开始，侬拿剧情交我介绍介绍好哦?

485. I'll buy a synopsis first, then I'll explain things as you read it.
 我先去买份说明书，侬一面看，我一面讲拨侬听。

486. I am told it's very difficult to understand the words in Beijing Opera, is that so?
 听说京戏蛮难听懂格，是哦?

487. Yes, it is. But don't worry. There are captions to help you.
 是格。不过侬勿要担心，侬可以看字幕。

488. Is it a Mei-style or Cheng-style opera?
 迪个是梅派戏还是程派戏?

489. It seems you know a lot about Beijing Opera.
 看来侬对京戏是蛮内行格。

490. Not really. I've read a little about it.
 谈不上内行，只是从书本浪向了解到一点点。

491. When will it start?
 戏几点钟开始?

492. At seven sharp. Let's go now.
 七点正。走吧。

493. How did you like the show?

侬觉得做得哪能?

494. Wonderful! I enjoyed the acting very much. I also liked the costumes. I was fascinated by them.

太崭了!我邪气欣赏演员格表演,特别是伊拉格服装,简直使我入迷了.

Part 2

Going To The Movies

看 电 影

495. What's on at the Guotai Theater tonight?

今朝夜里,国泰电影院放啥个片子?

496. It's "Shaolin Temple", a feature in technicolor.

彩色故事片《少林寺》.

497. We had better go and get the tickets at once.

阿拉快点去买票.

498. I've already gotten the tickets. They are very good. Seats 2 and 4, Row 14 in the lower section.

我已经买好了.位子老好格.楼下14排2座交4座.

499. Who is the director?

导演是啥人?

500. In this film not only is the color marvellous, but the scenery is beautiful, too.

迪部片子色彩嗲，风景也邪气漂亮。

501. And how good the music is!

音乐也蛮好听格。

502. It has an intricate and moving plot.

故事情节又曲折又动人。

503. I really want to see it again.

我真想再看一遍。

Part 3

Watching Television

看电视

504. What are you doing?

侬拉拉做啥？

505. I'm reading the "Television Weekly".

我拉拉看《电视周报》。

506. What programs are on TV tonight?

今朝夜里有啥电视节目？

507. On channel 5, from 7 to half past 7, it will be the news. After half past 7, it will be "Cultural Life" and "Glimpses of Our Motherland".

五频道七点到七点半是"新闻联播"，七点半以后是"文化生活"搭之"祖国各地"节目。

508. What about channel 8?
八频道有啥节目?

509. Channel 8 will televise a soccer match live.
八频道是足球比赛实况转播。

510. Which teams are playing?
是阿里两个队比赛?

511. It's between teams from Shanghai and Hong Kong.
上海队对香港队。

512. Excellent! It must be very exciting.
好极了!一定邪气精彩。

513. Who do you think will win?
侬看啥人会赢?

514. Hard to tell. They've won in the past. Last year Shanghai won.
蛮难讲。过去比赛互有胜负,旧年上海队赢了。

515. What was the score of that match?
伊场比赛格比分是多少?

516. The score was one to nothing, but this year Hong Kong beat Shanghai three to one.
比分是一比零。但是今年上海队以一比三输拨了香港队。

517. I'm sure it will be a close contest. Please come over and we will watch it together.

我敢肯定,迭场比赛一定邪气激烈。夜道侬到我格搭来,阿拉一道看。

LESSON 15

TRAVELING
旅 行

Part 1

Going Through The Formalities Of Traveling
办理旅行手续

518. I'm going to visit other parts of the country next month.
我打算下个号头到外地去旅行。

519. Are you going alone or are you traveling with a group?
侬自家去还是跟旅行团一道去?

520. What's the difference in the formalities?
办手续有啥不同哦?

521. If you are taking the trip with a group, the formalities will be taken care of by the Travel Service.
假定交旅行团一道去,手续可以由旅行社代办。

522. If I'm going alone, what should I do?
假定我自家去,哪能办呢?

523. You should take your passport and go to the Foreign Affairs Section of the Public Security Bureau of the city to get a travel permit.
侬应该带好护照到市公安局外事科办理签证。

524. Please fill in the Foreign Visitor's Application Form.
请填一张外国人旅行申请表。

525. Tell me your itinerary, please.
请告诉我侬格旅行路线。

526. I'll be leaving Beijing for Hangzhou, via Nanjing and Shanghai.
我从北京出发,经过南京,上海,到杭州。

527. Do you have any family members traveling together with you?
有家属一道去哦?

528. My wife and my daughter.
有我格夫人搭之囡囡。

529. How many days will this trip take?
侬准备旅行几天?

530. It will take about 20 days.
大约廿天。

531. We'll contact you by telephone as soon as the formalities are completed.
手续办好后,阿拉会得打电话告诉侬格。

532. The service charge is three yuan.
请交三块洋钿手续费。

Part 2

Traveling by Train
乘火车

533. Which train should I take for Guangzhou, please?

请问,到广州去应该乘阿里一趟火车?

534. You'd better take the express No. 15.

侬最好乘15次特快。

535. Give me a soft berth of Guangzhou, please.

我买一张到广州格软卧票。

536. How long is the ticket valid?

车票格有效期是几天?

537. Is it possible for me to make a stopover in Wuhan for one day?

拉拉武汉停一天可以哦?

538. Yes, but you have to get the ticket endorsed at the Wuhan Station.

可以,请侬拉拉武汉站签票。

539. How much luggage can I take with me?

我随身可以带多少公斤格行李?

540. How much does one pay for excess luggage?

行李超重每公斤要付几钿?

541. Where can I have my luggage checked?
垃拉啥地方办理行李托运?

542. Where is the waiting room?
候车室垃拉啥地方?

543. Excuse me. When does the train leave?
请问,迪趟火车几点钟开?

544. What platform does the train leave from?
迪趟火车垃拉阿里一个月台开出?

545. Give your ticket to the conductor, please.
请拿车票交拨列车员。

546. Excuse me. Where is the Chief Conductor (dining-car)?
请问,列车长(餐车)垃拉啥地方?

547. Is our train going to be late?
迪趟火车有勿有晚点?

548. How long does the train stop here?
火车垃拉迪搭要停几化辰光?

549. Please wake me one hour before arrival.
请垃到站格前一个钟头叫醒我。

Part 3

Traveling by Ship
乘 船

550. Excuse me. Do you have a sailing list with full particulars?
请问, 详细格船期时刻表有哦?

551. I want to book a ticket for Qingdao.
我要订一张去青岛格船票。

552. How much is a 1st (2nd) class ticket?
头等舱(二等舱)格价钿是几化?

553. When will we start boarding?
啥个辰光开始上船?

554. How many days does it take to get to Qingdao?
到青岛, 船要开几天?

555. At which dock should I go to board?
垃拉阿里一个码头上船?

556. Are there foreign language books and newspapers in the lounge?
休息厅里有外文书搭之报纸哦?

557. I feel sick and I think I'm going to vomit. Do you have any medicine for seasickness?
我觉得不适宜, 想呕, 晕船药有哦?

Part 4

Traveling by Plane
乘飞机

558. I'd like to book two tickets on the plane to Athens for Tuesday.
我要预定两张礼拜二到雅典格飞机票。

559. Do you want one-way or return tickets?
是单程票还是来回票?

560. Does our teenager have to pay the adult fare?
十几岁格小人是勿是也要买全票?

561. When will CAAC Flight 981 for New York take off?
请问,飞往纽约格中国民航981次班机啥辰光起飞?

562. What time should I be at the airport?
我应该几点钟到机场?

563. Is the weather okay for flying today?
今朝格天气飞机能起飞哦?

564. How long will our flight be delayed?
飞机起飞格辰光要推迟多少?

565. Which gate should I go to for CAAC Flight 303?
上中国民航格303次班机,从阿里一个门走?

566. Please go to Gate No. 5.
请到五号门等候。

567. How many hours does it take to fly from Shanghai to Tokyo?
从上海到东京要飞几个钟头?

568. Ladies and gentlemen, the plane is ready to take off. Please fasten your seat belts.
旅客们请注意,飞机马上要起飞了,请大家结好安全带。

569. Please refrain from smoking.
请勿要吃香烟

570. May I smoke now?
现在可以吃香烟了哦?

571. Where do we stop over on the way?
中途垃啥地方降落?

572. We'll stay in Karachi for an hour.
垃拉卡拉奇停一个钟头。

573. What altitude (speed) are we flying at?
现在飞格高度(速度)是多少?

574. I'm not feeling well. Could I stretch out on those two empty seats?

我勿大适宜，可以垃拉伊面两只空位子浪向睏一歇哦？

575. Ladies and gentlemen, we shall land in Paris in five minutes, be sure to take your things with you.

各位旅客，再过五分钟，就要到巴黎了。请大家带好自家格末事。

LESSON 16

LEAVE-TAKING
告 别

Part 1

At A Farewell Banquet
拉拉告别宴会上

576. It was very kind of you to have invited me.
邪气感谢侬格盛情邀请。

577. It's a pleasure to have you here.
欢迎光临。

578. We feel greatly honored to be invited to this banquet. We'd like to express our thanks to our hosts for their kind hospitality.
今朝我能参加格能介格宴会,感到十分荣幸。对主人格盛情款待,表示衷心格感谢。

579. We are very glad to have the opportunity to meet Mr. Brown in China.
阿拉交布朗先生能有机会拉拉中国碰面,真是邪气开心。

580. How time flies. Here we are saying good-bye already.
辰光过得真快,阿拉马上就要再会了。

581. I've spent a wonderful month here. It's really hard for me to part from you.

迪个一个号头,我过得邪气开心,现在实在舍不得交倻分别。

582. China has left a deep impression on me.

中国拨我留下了很深格印象。

583. In the past month we didn't look after you well enough and there were shortcoming in our arrangements, too. I hope you'll excuse us.

垃拉迪个一个号头里,阿拉对侬照顾得勿够好,活动安排也有交关勿周到格地方,请侬多多原谅。

584. This is an informal gathering among friends. Please make yourselves at home.

今朝是朋友道理个聚会,希望大家才勿要客气。

585. Well, what would you prefer, Maotai or wine?

哪能呀?侬是欢喜茅台还是欢喜葡萄酒?

586. Now let me propose a toast to the friendship between our two peoples.

现在我提议,为阿拉两国人民格友谊干杯!

587. Here's to the health of Comrade Lu and also to the health of everyone present.

为陆同志搭之在座格各位先生格健康干杯!

588. Come on, have one more glass.

来,再吃一杯。

589. No, thank you, I can't drink any more.

不,谢谢,勿能再吃了。

Part 2

Saying Good-bye At The Airport
机场送行

590. I'm touched by your coming to see me off even though you're so busy.

    㑚拉百忙当中来送我，使我邪气感动。

591. I'm sorry I couldn't find time to say good-bye to Comrade Liu. Will you be kind enough to thank him for me?

    我来勿及交刘同志告别，感到邪气抱歉。请侬向伊转达我格谢意。

592. I hope you'll have another opportunity to visit China in the future.

    我希望侬能有机会再到中国来看看。

593. I'm sure we'll meet again.

    我相信阿拉一定会得再碰面格。

594. We hope we'll have the opportunity to meet our Chinese friends in our country.

    阿拉希望将来能有机会垃拉阿拉国家欢迎中国朋友。

595. We'll certainly call on you if we have an opportunity to visit your country.

    假定有机会到贵国去旅行，阿拉一定去拜访侬。

596. Please write to us often.

    请侬经常来信。

597. I'll write to you as soon as I get back home.
我回国以后，马上就给你写信。

598. The plane is about to take off. Please get ready to board.
飞机就要起飞了，请准备上飞机。

599. Bon voyage!
祝你一路平安！

600. Please give our regards to your family!
请向你家里各人问好！